CREATIVE WAYS TO LOVE ENCOURAGE HER

MILITARY EDITION

JEFFERSON BETHKE

Unless otherwise noted, Scriptures are taken from the Holy Bible, New International Version®, NIV®. Copyright © 1973, 1978, 1984, 2011 by Biblica, Inc.™ Used by permission from Zondervan. All rights reserved worldwide. www.zondervan.com.

The Library of Congress Cataloging-in-Publication
Data is on file with the Library of Congress
IISBN-13: 978-0692997604

HOW TO GET THE MOST OUT OF THIS BOOK.

First off, you rock. By getting these paired books and wanting to go through them with your significant other, you obviously are already dominating at life! We have prayed over this project and really believe it can be a fun way to cultivate a healthy relationship. It can also bring back the joy and intimacy that sometimes gets lost amidst the everyday activities and the specific stresses of military life.

We've received an overwhelming response from military couples that wanted relationship resources, but because of the uniqueness of their life, needed guidance that would work well in their specific context.

We jumped at the chance to offer support and encouragement to military couples! So, we took some of our own ideas and practices that we've loved incorporating into our own marriage, and we also polled amazing military couples and asked them to contribute some of their own ideas for staying connected despite separation and stress.

After hearing the incredible stories of military couples scattered all over the world, we learned a few things about you. First, we learned that military marriage is hard. Like, really hard. And here's the other things we learned: military marriages are resilient. You stare down PCS moves, workups, deployments, trauma, loss, loneliness, and constant change. And you do it together, as a team. We are in awe!

Our goal in this book is to provide in-depth, practical, as well as light-hearted ideas to keep you turning toward each other, even when the momentum of military life separates you.

To get the most out of this book, we'd say: lean in. Lean into the ideas, the spontaneity, and the parts that stretch you the most. Don't be afraid to just go for it, have fun, and create memories. We are firm believers that with these two books, like so much in life, whatever you put into it, you will get out of it.

Also, this is just a template. Some things won't be the right fit for your relationship, your current season, or your resources. We have tried to make every day as applicable for you as possible. But with that said, feel free to morph, change, adapt, and do whatever you need to do to get the most out of each and every entry. At the end of the day, the goal isn't to follow this book rigidly and "cross each day off your checklist." Instead, our goal is to help you bring a fresh vibrancy and life to your relationship.

We are honored to offer this resource to you and we do so humbly with so much gratitude for the sacrifices you make to serve our country. We appreciate you!

JEFF & ALYSSA BETHKE

P.S. A quick note to the dating folks out there: Obviously we are married, so we are coming from that perspective. We designed the book inclusive of dating couples as much as we could, so you could find it useful, too. As mentioned above, you might have to morph it in a different way to fit your specific circumstances. We encourage you to make it your own and hope you will revisit the contents again when you're married!

P.P.S. You can learn more about our amazing contributing couples at the end of the 31 Days entries. You will be inspired by their stories...we are so grateful for their participation and wisdom!

DAY ONE: PRAYER

Some of the most encouraging times ever in our marriage are when Alyssa tells me she's praying for me. Not just in general but when she tells me the specifics of her prayer: she's praying for my walk with Jesus, she's praying I'd come to know Him in a deeper way that day, she's praying for my purity, she's praying that God would protect and guard my thoughts and mind, or she's praying that God would give me wisdom in how to parent. And the list goes on!

It makes me feel like I'm not alone. On the bad days or the hard days or the days when I feel shame or temptation, her prayers remind me I have an advocate. Not only is Alyssa in my corner, but most of all, Jesus is. He stands with me and for me.

Make a point to ask your wife or girlfriend how she could use prayer. Then sometime over the next week write a prayer out for her on a card or send it in an email or text. If you are together, or you have the option to talk on the phone, simply ask her if you can pray for her out loud.

If you need an idea for how to incorporate prayer for your wife or girlfriend into your daily rhythm, especially during times apart, you can borrow this cool idea from seasoned Navy couple, Rich and Nicole Schmaeling: No matter where they are in the world, no matter how far apart, they take a moment to pray for each other when they see the sunset.

JOURNAL BELOW:

WRITE WHAT YOU LEARNED TODAY, HOW IT
WENT AND WHAT MEMORIES WERE MADE.

DAY TWO: THOUGHT-FULNESS

Alyssa and I just had our second child in 2016. When we were in the hospital, as the dad, I did a good amount of sitting around. I don't know about you, but when I sit around I basically just want to eat. Food. And lots of it.

Alyssa could sense this and told me to open her overnight bag. When I looked in it, I saw a few of my favorite snacks (peanut butter M&M's for those wondering). And I immediately felt so loved. Why? Because I was thought of beforehand. It probably took Alyssa 80 cents at the grocery store the week before and about 15 seconds of extra attention. That's all it cost. It was this tiny moment of feeling special and understood, like she knew me. (Well, also because I get hungry, so I guess it was in her best interest to keep me fed, too.)

My wife knows the things that will speak my language. To some, words are everything. To others, actions are what really communicate. Apparently, I'm just a sucker for peanut butter M&M's. The trick is to spend some time thinking about what really speaks to your partner.

Navy couple, David and Becky Hammond, shared with us about the vast differences between how they each experience love and thoughtfulness. This is true of most couples!

David says: "Because we know that we both receive love in such different ways, we are continuously aware of the intentionality it takes to truly see and care for each other--deployment or not! It's important to know what really feeds your wife's soul and do that, even if it takes some creativity."

Think of something your girl loves. Her favorite treat. Or coffee drink. Words she wants to hear from you. Her favorite flower. A helpful chore. Or something else that communicates you're thinking of her. Surprise her with it. If you aren't together, send a surprise via Amazon (Amazon always has your back!) to her doorstep or office. When she asks why? Say, "No reason, I was just thinking of you."

JOURNAL BELOW:

WRITE WHAT YOU LEARNED TODAY, HOW IT
WENT AND WHAT MEMORIES WERE MADE.

_____

_____

_____

_____

_____

_____

_____

_____

_____

_____

_____

_____

_____

_____

DAY THREE: LAUGHTER

"Laughter is carbonated holiness."
-Anne Lamott

It's true! There's something about laughter that is downright sacred. When you're laughing, there's joy you can't explain. It does something to you: warms your heart, changes your body chemistry, and heals you from the outside, in. George Gordon Byron said it perfectly, "Always laugh when you can. It's cheap medicine." Ha!

It's an understatement to say Alyssa and I love to laugh. I'm always doing something dumb around the house. Making up a song of sorts or talking in these weird accents that I create. (Frankly, if anyone BUT Alyssa saw these antics, they'd probably think I was crazy.) I've started to realize that laughter connects us, brings us closer together, helps us relax and not take things too seriously. Cultivating joy can actually be like a bonding agent in a relationship. It makes the relationship stronger.

Laughter is essential in every relationship, but especially powerful in a military marriage where circumstances are intense and the stress is high. How can you make your woman laugh today? Maybe it's as simple as sending her an outrageous meme, making a funny video of yourself that she can watch while you're gone, or recording a silly song she can listen to when she's down. Send her a bag of Laffy Taffy, and have her read you her favorite joke from the wrappers. Even a good-natured prank can create a hilarious memory together.

Be creative! Your job is to put a giant smile on her face today!

JOURNAL BELOW:

WRITE WHAT YOU LEARNED TODAY, HOW IT
WENT AND WHAT MEMORIES WERE MADE.

DAY FOUR: COMMUNICATION

Yesterday Alyssa and I had a little fight. Or...disagreement is probably a better word, but you know what I mean. It was one of those times when you're both a little frustrated and you start getting a phrase in your head like, "I know I'm right. Why doesn't she _____?!" (You can fill in the blank.)

In the disagreement with Alyssa, when I really started to think about it, I realized what we were fighting about wasn't actually what were upset about. We ended up in a disagreement because we didn't properly communicate beforehand. And when you don't communicate, expectations aren't met and that's usually ground zero for tension, strife and frustration.

A lot of times, the disagreements aren't the actual problem. They are just the symptom. They are pointing to something earlier or previous that is the real culprit, the actual reason why there is frustration.

Ask your wife how you can communicate better. Ask her if there are any instances or things you say or do that frustrate her, if there are times when you didn't clearly communicate what you were hoping for. Rehash the past few disagreements or unmet expectations and ask how you could have communicated better before they happened in order for the same problem to not happen again. If you know what the disagreement was really about, the *real* reason you were fighting, talk about that too.

Navy couple, Rico and Heather Madaffari, are currently navigating their 8th (yes, 8th!) deployment. Rico talks about the importance of communication: It's simple, but also very challenging at times--honest communication. Open communication is so huge, especially in this lifestyle. The ability to be vulnerable with your spouse takes time, but it has been a vital part of our marriage.

Developing healthy communication is a cornerstone in every marriage, but especially when you don't always have non-verbal cues to go off of. Slowing down and communicating honestly before things get heated can really go a long way!

JOURNAL BELOW:

WRITE WHAT YOU LEARNED TODAY, HOW IT
WENT AND WHAT MEMORIES WERE MADE.

DAY FIVE: DANCE

Alyssa and I always have music on in the house. We usually turn worship music on in the morning and have it playing in the background through the day. But once it's dinnertime, especially if I decide to hop in the kitchen and cook, I like to listen to something with a little more funk.

This usually means Taylor Swift, Justin Timberlake, Bruno Mars and maybe some Justin Bieber. (Don't judge me . . . because I know you're thinking about judging me right now. Is it too late now to say sorry?) And when a good song comes on there's a good chance I'll grab Alyssa and start twirling her, dancing with her and giving her a little old school dip for the grand finale. My favorite part is that our toddler Kinsley absolutely loves it and giggles the whole time.

There's something about dancing that brings joy and life. So for today, dance with your girl. It can be a funky spontaneous dinner dance. It can be you turning something on in the car and getting out in the parking lot for a few minutes. It can mean going old school with some Macarena even. Most of all have fun with it; don't be afraid to let loose and dance away! If you know you have time apart coming up, video yourselves dancing—maybe one sweet slow dance and then an upbeat number, too. Give the video to her as a memory she can come back to while you're away.

JOURNAL BELOW:

WRITE WHAT YOU LEARNED TODAY, HOW IT
WENT AND WHAT MEMORIES WERE MADE.

_____

_____

_____

_____

_____

_____

_____

_____

_____

_____

_____

_____

_____

DAY SIX: FORGIVENESS

Recently Alyssa and I got into one of those little disagreements. You know, the ones where by the time you get to the end of it, you can't really even remember why you were arguing in the first place.

This one was definitely my fault. I had made a dumb side comment that was meant to be funny but in retrospect was just snarky and hurtful. When I made the comment, we were in the grocery store and just about to part ways to divide and conquer our shopping list (the only right way to do it, especially with kids, CAN I GET AN AMEN). Once I went off to tackle my part of the list, I had a few minutes to think on what I said and how I said it. You know what I realized? It was simply my fault. I was wrong and what I said was hurtful. I immediately felt bad and realized I needed to apologize and ask for forgiveness. A couple minutes later once we reconvened, I said I was sorry. I asked her to forgive me.

Then it hit me—forgiveness truly is one of the sustaining powers of a relationship. Without it, surely every relationship would venture into realms of resentment, hurt, bitterness and even division. Those toxic dynamics can destroy a relationship. I'd say hands down one reason I feel like Alyssa and I have a relatively healthy relationship is we both consider apologies and forgiveness to be non-negotiable. We believe that one of us must be humble enough to apologize and one must be gracious enough to accept and speak forgiveness.

Think of one thing you haven't apologized for that you said, did or held onto today, yesterday or maybe even long ago. Ask your wife or girlfriend to forgive you. Don't be so proud that you're unwilling to go first.

JOURNAL BELOW:

WRITE WHAT YOU LEARNED TODAY, HOW IT
WENT AND WHAT MEMORIES WERE MADE.

_____

_____

_____

_____

_____

_____

_____

_____

_____

_____

_____

_____

_____

_____

DAY SEVEN: MUSIC

Alyssa and I were both teenagers, coming of age, at the end of the 90's and beginning of the 2000's. Because of this, we were in the glory days for music playlists. Back then a playlist wasn't just something you made quickly on your iPhone. It was actually incredibly thought out and structured. You then burned it onto a CD for your significant other. (Please tell me I'm not the only one remembering this right now.)

Now, I don't want to be the person who is always like, "Well, back in MY DAY," trapped in classic dad syndrome. But something special has been lost with the dying art of making music mixes for each other. I, to this day, still remember a few different ones I made Alyssa while we were dating and even one I made during our break-up that I gave to her after we got back together.

Music is one of those things that instantly connects you, even across the miles. Submariner Matthew Colter knew he would be almost completely out of touch during his deployment, so he wanted to find creative ways to be present with his wife, Krista, even though he was gone. Matthew says: "*I created a playlist with all the songs that I loved singing to her. She loved the playlist and told me she listened to it almost every day.*"

Whether it's an iPhone playlist or an actual CD you burn, make your girl a playlist today. Be thoughtful with the theme. Choose songs that remind you of her, that tell your story from the beginning, or songs you hope represent your relationship. And if an entire playlist is too ambitious, choose a song—call it "our song"—for you to both come back to, especially when you're not together.

JOURNAL BELOW:

WRITE WHAT YOU LEARNED TODAY, HOW IT
WENT AND WHAT MEMORIES WERE MADE.

DAY EIGHT: HOW CAN I SUPPORT YOU?

Over and over, we heard from our military couples about the importance of getting support for the person at home. Practical, hands-on help, seemed to be always appreciated (and often needed).

Navy Pilot Rich Schmaeling talks about supporting his wife, Nicole, while he was deployed: *"I always tried to be supportive of her getting a babysitter for our three kids whenever she felt like she needed a break."*

Today, ask your wife or girlfriend what kind of support would be helpful to her in this season. Does she need a house cleaner to come twice a month? Does she need a babysitter? Does she need a weekend getaway with girlfriends? Does she need someone to help her take care of the lawn?

Let her know you don't expect her to handle everything on her own and encourage her to get the support she needs. This communicates you care and you don't have unrealistic expectations of her. Remember to tell her that she is strong and capable and it's OK to ask for help, too.

Your village wants to support as well! Of course no one can love and encourage your wife or girlfriend quite like you can because no one shares the same intimacy you do. But one of the ways you can really buoy her is to reach out to friends and family and remind them to send her a note or a text of encouragement or invite her to do something she loves to do.

In your absence, she needs nurture and, even, distractions at times. Friends and family always want to help, but sometimes they don't know how. Cueing them to contact your wife or girlfriend—even reminding them of special dates or occasions (for example, the one month mark after you've left)—will give your community constructive ways to support your marriage even when you can't be there.

JOURNAL BELOW:

WRITE WHAT YOU LEARNED TODAY, HOW IT
WENT AND WHAT MEMORIES WERE MADE.

_____

_____

_____

_____

_____

_____

_____

_____

_____

_____

_____

_____

_____

_____

DAY
NINE:
NOTES

Sticky notes are the best invention ever! They are good for to-do lists, daily reminders, and pranking a friend by putting them all over their car (or is that just me). Each new day brings an opportunity to speak words that build up or words that tear down. And each day is an opportunity to speak a new set of encouraging words. Alyssa and I do this a million different ways: sometimes I leave sticky notes around the house with things on each of them that I enjoy, appreciate, or admire about her.

So think of the top 10 traits or qualities you love about your wife or girlfriend. Write them down on separate pieces of paper. Then put them all over any place she'd normally see them in a day. For example, put one on the nightstand, one where she gets coffee in the cupboard, one on her speedometer in her car, etc.

If you are long-distance, send her one thing you love about her each hour, on the hour, throughout her day for 10 hours! Or, if you know you're deploying, steal this genius idea from Rico Madaffari: "*The first couple weeks of deployment are always the hardest on my wife. So I leave post-it notes around the house before I go. I try not to leave them in the most obvious places—maybe hide one in the medicine cabinet or deep in a drawer. The notes are short, sometimes just a few encouraging words, or even just, "I miss you." Heather usually finds them all by the end of the first month, but that's when she needs the encouragement the most. Even though these notes don't take that much time, they always mean a lot to her.*"

JOURNAL BELOW:

WRITE WHAT YOU LEARNED TODAY, HOW IT
WENT AND WHAT MEMORIES WERE MADE.

_____

_____

_____

_____

_____

_____

_____

_____

_____

_____

_____

_____

_____

DAY TEN: STORIES

Stories are powerful. Whether we realize it or not, we think in story. We are not mindless computers absorbing data. We give that data flesh. The data gets humanized. It gets storied. And a lot of times, story is the very way we remember our past and look towards the future. As a couple, we know this is true. We don't see our relationship as random abstract things but instead as the crazy story of how two lives intersected and were never the same again.

I mean, if you've been together for any length of time, you know getting asked your story is something you almost begin to memorize. I realized the other day that every time I tell the story of how Alyssa and I met and married, I feel this little spark of joy and gratitude that I ended up with her. There's something about recounting your story that gives your relationship strength: the good, the bad, the easy, the hard, the breakup, the kids, the first date, or that awkward first kiss. Which Alyssa and I definitely had. But that's a story for another time.

Spend some time going back over your story today. Ask your wife or girlfriend to retell it in her own words. There's always more to learn and hear, so try to ask questions and listen like it's the first time you've heard the story. Talk about the hard times you've endured so far. Talk about the good times you've enjoyed so far. Then, and this is the best part in my opinion, talk about what your story will sound like and look like in, say, 10 years. What do you want your story to be then?

JOURNAL BELOW:

WRITE WHAT YOU LEARNED TODAY, HOW IT
WENT AND WHAT MEMORIES WERE MADE.

_____

_____

_____

_____

_____

_____

_____

_____

_____

_____

_____

_____

_____

DAY ELEVEN: BRING HOME A TREAT

My girl, Alyssa loves flowers and coffee. She doesn't need elaborate arrangements; she loves even just one sunflower. And I know her coffee order by heart! I try to bring flowers home to her regularly or bring her a coffee when she's not expecting it. Bringing home a treat is always a good idea!

If you've been someplace exotic, bring your wife or girlfriend something unique and interesting that represents the culture you've been in. It can help bring her into your experience even though she wasn't there with you. Share the story of buying it and why you chose that particular item for her. It doesn't need to be expensive, but rather something that holds a story or says, "I know you."

You can also stop in the airport duty free shops on your way home and pick up her favorite chocolates or perfume. These are gestures that foster connection, gratitude, and intimacy.

JOURNAL BELOW:

WRITE WHAT YOU LEARNED TODAY, HOW IT WENT AND WHAT MEMORIES WERE MADE.

_____

_____

_____

_____

DAY TWELVE: ESCAPE TOGETHER

Love and appreciation can be communicated in all kinds of ways. Words, special surprises, taking on a task for the other person...these are all ways we can express our love and appreciation. But when all else fails, here's a great way to connect: Escape together!

Sometimes extended and expensive getaways aren't possible. I love what dual military couple, Melissa Reyes and her boyfriend, do to escape together: *"We both suffer from anxiety and PTSD due to our time in the military. If we are upset, not in a good mood, or we just need time together, we get on his motorcycle and we ride at least 30 minutes to an hour. We have an escape, something we both do together that's our thing."*

Instead of choosing time alone, what's something you can invite your girl to do that would serve as an escape for you both, especially if you're feeling stressed or disconnected? Here are a few ideas for activities you can do that will help you clear your minds together:

- Go to the batting cages
- Go on a walk or run
- Plant a garden or work in the yard
- Go horseback riding
- Go on a bike ride
- Cook a meal together or attend a cooking class
- Get a couples massage
- Go to the driving range
- Pack a picnic
- Visit a theme park and ride the roller coasters

Think of escaping together as a "time out" from the pressures and stress of reality. Brainstorm an escape—for an hour, a morning, or a half-day—that would be mutually refreshing to both of you and a way for you to reset together.

JOURNAL BELOW:

WRITE WHAT YOU LEARNED TODAY, HOW IT
WENT AND WHAT MEMORIES WERE MADE.

DAY THIRTEEN: HER WORLD

I absolutely love *Back To The Future*. It's my favorite movie of all time. In my office I have a Back To The Future poster, Marty and Doc figurines, as well as a now discontinued DeLorean Lego set. To say I'm a fan is an understatement. In fact, I always know other fans based on my constant use of one-liners from the film. ("There's that word again, heavy. Is there something wrong with the earth's gravitational pull in the future?") I know when someone *isn't* a fan if I drop a line and they just stare blankly.

When I got married, I wanted to see if my wife was a BTTF fan too but to my surprise, she hadn't seen the movie yet. We ended up watching it on our honeymoon. I remember watching it with Alyssa and being able to tell she thought it was fun and a good movie, but she didn't think it was life changing, like I did. If my memory serves me correctly, we've even watched it since then. Alyssa isn't a huge fan but keeps watching it. Why? Because she wants to enter into my world. She wants to know the one-liners so she can use them with me. She wants to watch the movie because she wants to get that much closer to me.

Entering into the world of your wife or girlfriend is vital to a healthy relationship. It always saddens me when I see a couple who has a "he does his thing, she does her thing" type of relationship. Healthy couples enter into each other's spaces. How can you enter her world today?

When you are apart, and you are literally in different worlds, spend some time thinking about her day. What is her routine, her responsibilities, her pressures, her stresses? What might it be like to be in her shoes? How could you enter her world even when it doesn't feel like you're a part of it?

Research one of her interests, so you could ask her meaningful questions about it. Or, acknowledge some of the details of her day that she may not be expecting you to think about. Or, send her a coupon for a couples' pedicure, redeemable anytime upon your return. This one really isn't all that bad even though us guys hate on it. Someone cleaning my feet, making them look good and then ending it all with a foot massage—fine by me!

JOURNAL BELOW:

WRITE WHAT YOU LEARNED TODAY, HOW IT
WENT AND WHAT MEMORIES WERE MADE.

_____

_____

_____

_____

_____

_____

_____

_____

_____

_____

_____

_____

_____

_____

DAY FOUR- TEEN: YOUR WORLD

Yesterday, you took some time to put yourself in "her world," to think about the details of her day and intentionally enter into her reality. Today is about letting her into "your world."

Our wives and girlfriends want to know what's going on in our hearts, minds, and lives. Sometimes we assume they know what we're thinking about, what our day looks like, what stresses we're facing, but I've found that it's important to actually talk about those things.

Alyssa loves to go on walks, and she goes on one almost every day. She always invites me to go with her, but in the past I wasn't that into it. I decided—because she loves it so much—to start going on these walks with her. I've realized that the walks lead to good conversations between us and offer an opportunity for me to let her into my world a bit more.

As a military couple, you don't always have the opportunity to let her into your world entirely. Because of distance, security, or other logistics, sometimes it can feel like you are on different planets. That's why it's so important to be intentional with what you can share so she feels like she can get glimpses into your day.

Air Force Major Brian Witthoeft talks about how he made this happen: *"One of the most important things for us during deployments and other separations is video chat. It is helpful to see each other as we talked. And for the kids it was especially helpful. I think the transition home was easier for them because of video chat. My wife appreciated hearing about the people I work with, the food I eat, and what the location looked like. It helped her "picture" life for me."*

Think of three details from "your world" that you could share with your girl today—specifics about the culture you're in or the experience you're having while away from her, something you're thinking about, or a funny story that happened to you at work. It doesn't have to be all that deep or serious; it just needs to be a window into "your world," only for her.

JOURNAL BELOW:

WRITE WHAT YOU LEARNED TODAY, HOW IT
WENT AND WHAT MEMORIES WERE MADE.

_____

_____

_____

_____

_____

_____

_____

_____

_____

_____

_____

_____

_____

DAY FIFTEEN: DREAMS

Alyssa and I were only dating at the time but I remember when she started to mention how she was looking to find a new hobby. Photography was something she mentioned as one of those possible hobbies, so I filed that away and waited. I waited to see if any of the particular hobbies she mentioned bubbled back up. And again photography did. She talked about how she really wanted to start getting into it but didn't have a camera. The problem is I was broke and couldn't buy her a camera. She had a good steady job though and soon enough, she bought herself a camera. A few months went by and she started to get really into it, but she didn't have that great of a lens.

I started saving. I had some photography friends I'd text and message asking them what they knew about quality lenses. Finally I bought a lens and surprised her with it. It has been so fun to watch her take pictures of families, high schoolers, kids, and so much more with that camera.

In a relationship, both people have dreams, hopes and future plans. Either a skill they wish they had, a class they wish they could take, or a piece of equipment they're saving for. Maybe your wife or girlfriend wants to get better at cooking. Maybe she wants to learn the guitar. Maybe she wants to start a garden at home. If you can think back on recurring themes over the past few months or years of your relationship, what would be one hobby or dream that she wants to pursue but hasn't gone for yet?

Whatever that answer is, today do something to encourage her toward her dream. Send her YouTube videos about learning the guitar. Or send her a cookbook you think she might enjoy. Send her a gift card to a local nursery or a pair of new gardening gloves. Then write her a note about how much you love to see her chase her passions and dreams and how you want to be her biggest cheerleader.

JOURNAL BELOW:

WRITE WHAT YOU LEARNED TODAY, HOW IT
WENT AND WHAT MEMORIES WERE MADE.

DAY SIXTEEN: SERVING

One of the best pieces of advice Alyssa and I ever got about marriage was to always remember that it's about giving, not taking. Or another way to put it is: marriage is about serving, not being served.

Think how much that latter one is true, even though we probably wouldn't admit it aloud. We structure our days, say certain things and do certain things in hopes that we would get served or that we would get what we want. Secretly, if our girlfriend or wife doesn't do those things we start to get resentful or contemptuous. We foster that toxic inner dialogue: *"She should...if only she...I can't believe she expects me to always..."*

One of the biggest joys of life is to get to serve your wife or girlfriend. Service is actually secretly the key to joy. I say "secretly" because most people haven't discovered this truth yet. Sure it takes a little bit more time and energy and sure, sometimes it feels harder than being served. But not many people—once they've done something special for someone else—think, "Well that was a total waste of time." No. We realize it did something in us. It created joy, not only for the person we served, but in us too.

Do one act of service today for your girlfriend or wife. For me, this usually means I make the bed, give her a back rub, or give the kiddos a bath. Whatever it is, serve her and then tell her how much of a joy it is to serve her.

If you're not at home, think of a way you could serve her from afar: whether that's ordering something and having it sent to her, hiring someone to help her out, sending her a prayer you're praying for her, or making a point to check in with her more regularly.

David Hammond shares how he did this: *"My wife, Becky, feels loved and encouraged through service, specifically hands-on help, chores, and tasks—hard to do from a distance! Because I couldn't be the hands and feet, I asked others to be the hands and feet instead. Becky and I discussed what "service" things we could hire out—housecleaning, babysitters, massage, acupuncture, a night away for her, or trips to visit her family for their hands-on help."*

Becky remembers hitting her limit one night. She says: "*The ship tour was unexpected, we had two kids under four and one due while he was gone, my mom was dying of brain cancer, and life was full in every way. I look back now and see how helpless David must have felt. Instead, he let me cry and helped put a couple live-giving acts of service in place— house cleaning and pregnancy massage. It didn't change my situation, but it did help me feel supported and encouraged and deeply known by my guy who was off doing something he not only loved but was truly made for.*"

With some creative thinking and planning, David was able to serve his wife in an unbelievable way even while he was on the other side of the world. Rockstar!

JOURNAL BELOW:

WRITE WHAT YOU LEARNED TODAY, HOW IT WENT AND WHAT MEMORIES WERE MADE.

_____

_____

_____

_____

_____

_____

_____

_____

DAY SEVEN- TEEN: LISTEN

By nature, I'm a fixer. I like to tinker with things, take them apart, put them back together. When something doesn't go the way I planned, I start analyzing it and wondering *how I can fix it*. This is a good trait most of the time (you know, when I'm building something or trying to solve a problem). But if I'm not careful, this can be hurtful to Alyssa.

Whenever she is feeling down, something bad happened, or she just needs to talk, the last thing she wants me to do is to try to fix it. In fact, she'll literally say during some of our discussions, don't try to fix it, just *listen*. Of course I want to be helpful when I try to solve the problem, but I'm trying to be helpful on my terms, not hers.

When you truly love someone, you love them on their terms. Meaning you offer encouragement, blessing, love, and kind words, in a way that they best receive, not the way you best receive. For Alyssa, she really appreciates when I listen. She wants to feel listened to. Heard. Seen. (Shoot, I'm that way too. It's natural to want to really be heard.)

So how can you listen better today? Make a special point to not talk as fast. Ask double the amount of questions you usually do. Or say "Can you tell me more about that?" or "Why do you like that or feel that way?" If the conversation is difficult, be aware when you start to feel defensive.

I love what military wife, Kristen Strong, shares about how her husband David listened to her when they were separated by deployments. She says, "*David made it safe for me to be open and frank about my perception of our difficulties. This didn't mean I unleashed every unrestrained thought and frustration (although truth be told, I sometimes did this too). But I so appreciated having the safe place to speak openly about things from my vantage point.*"

Part of listening, as Kristen said so well, is creating a safe space for authentic conversation. Let your wife or girlfriend know that you won't try to fix anything. You just want to listen.

JOURNAL BELOW:

WRITE WHAT YOU LEARNED TODAY, HOW IT
WENT AND WHAT MEMORIES WERE MADE.

_____

_____

_____

_____

_____

_____

_____

_____

_____

_____

_____

_____

_____

_____

DAY EIGHTTEEN: CHANGE

"Consider how tough it is to change yourself and you'll understand what little chance you have in trying to change others."
-Jacob M. Braude

If that above quote isn't a smack in the face, I don't know what is. In a relationship, once the butterflies start wearing off, you start to notice things. You start to notice things that annoy you, bother you, frustrate you, and upset you about the other person (and they certainly start to notice those things about you). One of the temptations is to want to change the person. You think *if only they would change this one thing, life would be a lot easier or better.* And while that might be the case, you'll soon realize your efforts are probably futile.

Trying to change the other person for your benefit in a relationship only brings more hurt, pain and heartache. Now don't get me wrong, change is good and both of you will change over time, but Alyssa and I have both noticed change happens best through prayer and the Holy Spirit. Instead of Alyssa or I telling each other about something we think needs to change in the other person, we start praying for that person and ask God to either A) show them the area they need to change or B) show us where we have room for growth. Sometimes we want to change the other person because we're afraid to look at ourselves.

Think on one thing that you usually want to change about your wife or girlfriend. Now really dig deep and ask yourself how you could change on that issue? For example, I hate making the bed and Alyssa loves to make the bed. We fought about it off and on for a year in our marriage. I tried so hard to change her. And finally God convicted me and said if she wanted it made, then I should serve and love her in that way. So now it gets made every morning, and I haven't brought it up since.

JOURNAL BELOW:

WRITE WHAT YOU LEARNED TODAY, HOW IT
WENT AND WHAT MEMORIES WERE MADE.

_____

_____

_____

_____

_____

_____

_____

_____

_____

_____

_____

_____

DAY NINE-TEEN: COMPLI-MENTS

I've noticed lately that a compliment has different levels of power based on who is giving it. A stranger might compliment me, and I'm encouraged, but when Alyssa compliments me it does so much more. Why? Because I'm closest to Alyssa and she's the love of my life. When the person who loves you and knows you and sees all your strengths and weaknesses still compliments you, those words have power!

Robert Brault once said, "There is no effect more disproportionate to its cause than the happiness bestowed by a small compliment." Isn't that so true? It's the easiest thing to do, yet can bring such an enormous amount of blessing to a person. And Mark Twain even said, "I can live for two months on a good compliment." Words give life. They can encourage and build up.

Matthew Colter adds: "*Nothing makes my wife, Krista, feel loved more than an unexpected compliment, especially during months when we aren't able to talk due to my work on the submarine. I thought of a few ways I could encourage her despite our separation, and so I wrote her letters and put them in places she wouldn't find right away. She loved getting a handwritten compliment from me 4 or 5 months after I'd left.*"

Give compliments to your wife or girlfriend today, but try focusing on what you specifically appreciate about her in this season. The word "appreciate" means "being fully conscious of" and "to value," so your words to her could show her that you're fully conscious of the value she is bringing to your life, home, and relationship. If you can, write them down so that she can revisit them. These will be life-giving words she can return to well beyond the moment they are spoken.

JOURNAL BELOW:

WRITE WHAT YOU LEARNED TODAY, HOW IT
WENT AND WHAT MEMORIES WERE MADE.

_____

_____

_____

_____

_____

_____

_____

_____

_____

_____

_____

_____

_____

DAY TWENTY: HARDSHIPS

Harriet Ann Jacobs was famous for saying, "There are no bonds so strong as those which are formed by suffering together." If someone were to ask me what Alyssa and I have gone through in marriage that made us grow the most or strengthened our relationship, it would no doubt be the hard things. Seasons of long-distance, tight finances, tough news we got from a friend, etc. Every time, difficult seasons are hard when we're walking through them, but looking back, there is something special about hardships that actually act as glue when we go through together.

Of course, no one goes hunting for hardships. But we don't have to avoid them either. So many times in relationships we try to do everything in our power to take the easiest road, make the easiest decision or do whatever will cause the least amount of tension.

After listening to so many of your stories, I am more convinced than ever that hardship and stress—while daunting at times—can also create bonds between a man and a woman that nothing else can. Rich and Nicole Schmaeling say it perfectly: *"Military life continues to have seasons of give and take, adjustments to family and daily rhythms. It's definitely taught us a lot about trust, gratitude, and flexibility. It's brought daily, yearly, seasonal challenges that have shaped and molded us, humbled us, and made us stronger."*

What if instead of dreading hardships and struggle, we embraced them somehow, seeing that God was making something new and strong in our relationship? What if, when difficulties landed on our doorstep, we welcomed them as moments to grow together in a way that prosperity or success could never produce.

Today, talk with your wife or girlfriend about the hardships you've encountered together because of military life—not to dwell on the negative, but to remember what you've been through together. Talk about how these struggles have produced fruit and connection in your relationship.

JOURNAL BELOW:

WRITE WHAT YOU LEARNED TODAY, HOW IT
WENT AND WHAT MEMORIES WERE MADE.

_____

_____

_____

_____

_____

_____

_____

_____

_____

_____

_____

_____

_____

DAY TWENTY-ONE: WASH FEET

I still remember the day I proposed to Alyssa. I had my two friends go before us to a secluded beach where they set the scene before we got there. They put out rose petals, lit candles, and hung up pictures from our relationship lining the pathway down from the car to the beach.

And when I got down to the bottom, there was a blanket and a bottle of champagne. It's hard for me to remember every little detail because it was such a blur (and I was so nervous). One thing I do remember is that before I proposed, I got down on my knees, took out a thermos of warm water and a washcloth from my backpack and began to wash her feet. I then proceeded to tell her I wanted this to be a symbol of our relationship, of me serving her and lifting her up. And then I asked her to marry me.

There's something about foot washing that is incredibly humbling. It feels a little awkward, yet holy. It's been a picture of service for thousands of years, originating in antiquity where foot washing was more of a necessity in many desert climates. While it might not be functionally as needed today, it is still a powerful picture to show care and affection and humility.

After your next separation, make a point to wash your wife's feet. Tell her how much you appreciate all she has been doing to keep your relationship strong and your household going. Acknowledge that she has been carrying a big burden and washing her feet is your way of saying thank you and it matters.

JOURNAL BELOW:

WRITE WHAT YOU LEARNED TODAY, HOW IT
WENT AND WHAT MEMORIES WERE MADE.

DAY TWENTY-TWO: GRACE WINS

Grace means we believe the best about our partner when we could, instead, choose to assume the worst. If we enter into conversations, even arguments, with the assumption that we are "for" each other, things tend to be much more productive. When you have nothing else to go on except words on a screen—no tone of voice, no body language, no facial expressions—misinterpretation can happen so easily! Assuming the worst tends to lead nowhere fast. But grace always wins.

Brian and Meghan Witthoeft talk about ways they've extended grace to each other: "*We try to stay away from assumptions, especially during re-entry. We make it a point to talk through things: anything that's been moved around the house, new routines for the kids, any change we can think of that could create miscommunication.*"

Rico Madaffari told us he makes a point to follow his wife's lead when he returns from a deployment. Heather says: "*He is always ready to jump right in, but he also realizes he has missed a lot, and that things have changed in our daily lives. He's always very open to how things are done. I find that supportive and helpful. I have been in control the entire time he's been gone, so for him to want to follow my lead is very much appreciated.*"

Miscommunication is practically inevitable in a relationship, but we always have the choice to give grace to each other, to believe the best, to believe that our wife or girlfriend is actually "for" us and not against us. How can you infuse your communication with grace today? Ask God to help you resist the temptation to grab for control or make unhelpful assumptions, but instead to increase your capacity for understanding and empathy.

JOURNAL BELOW:

WRITE WHAT YOU LEARNED TODAY, HOW IT
WENT AND WHAT MEMORIES WERE MADE.

DAY TWENTY-THREE: THAT'S A GOOD QUESTION

The ease of technology can make us feel like we are more connected than we really are. During times of separation, even if we talk regularly, our conversations can devolve into logistics, and we have to make a point to go beyond business partner into heart connection.

Every conversation cannot be award winning, but try to make a point to ask your wife or girlfriend good questions when you can:
How are you really doing?
What's something you're looking forward to?
What have you been thinking about lately?
Is there anything you need from me?
Is there anything you wish I would ask you or talk to you about?

Good questions show a desire to connect on a level deeper than details and they express an interest in the layers of her life.

It's amazing how effective the right question can be at eliciting powerful conversations. I have found that just a simple question can show Alyssa I care and I'm concerned and I'm listening.

Many of our contributing military couples raved about the ease and fun of picking a Netflix series to watch together or a book to read together during deployments. This gave them something to talk about and share besides just the logistics of life. If your conversation is stalling or just needs some fresh input, watch the same series or read the same book and then think of a few questions you could ask your wife or girlfriend based on what you guys are watching or reading. *Which character do you like the best? What was your favorite part? What bothered you in the story?* These questions are a great jumping off point for quality conversation.

JOURNAL BELOW:

WRITE WHAT YOU LEARNED TODAY, HOW IT
WENT AND WHAT MEMORIES WERE MADE.

DAY TWENTY-FOUR: KINDNESS

When you first start dating, you're on your best behavior. You do things and say things to impress but also shower kindness on your special someone. For example, it's common gentlemen etiquette to open the door for her, pull out her chair, bring flowers, and more.

For some reason if you've been dating or married for any length of time, this thoughtfulness starts to fade. But shouldn't it be the opposite? If the love and connection is growing, shouldn't those gestures at least stay the same or grow as well?

I know for me, I get really comfortable with Alyssa and I assume, "Oh, she knows how much I love her." Then I get complacent. She does know how I feel about her, but active pursuit is different than complacency. One leads to a flourishing relationship and one leads to fizzle.

Today, ask yourself what one thing you did when you were dating that you could reinstate now. What small gesture can you do to show her you're pursuing her and not becoming complacent?

Here's how that looked for Matthew Colter: "*I made a big deal for holidays, knowing I'd be out to sea during them. I set up gifts or flowers with quirky notes to arrive on those special days to remind her she is loved and always on my mind.*"

JOURNAL BELOW:

WRITE WHAT YOU LEARNED TODAY, HOW IT
WENT AND WHAT MEMORIES WERE MADE.

_____

_____

_____

_____

_____

_____

_____

_____

_____

_____

_____

_____

_____

DAY TWENTY-FIVE: CHEESY PICK-UP LINES

I'm a big fan of cheesiness. I'm the king of bad jokes and I love the most ridiculous pick-up lines. Just ask Alyssa. At this point she just barely laughs and makes a face that somewhat communicates, "Man, I sure got lucky marrying this guy."

My favorite thing to do is to surprise her with pick-up lines or bad jokes all throughout the day, especially when she least expects it. We haven't even gotten out of bed and I'll say, "Do you have a band-aid? Because I scraped my knee falling for you."

There's something about these dumb lines that brings a joy and spontaneity to our relationship that is really fun. I love to make her laugh, and when you can make your wife or girlfriend laugh, there's nothing better.

The task for today is to hop on Google and find 10 of your favorite cheesy pick-up lines, and then spread them out throughout the day. You can tell them to her face-to-face, write them down, or text them to her. Watch out! She will probably fall in love with you all over again!

JOURNAL BELOW:

WRITE WHAT YOU LEARNED TODAY, HOW IT WENT AND WHAT MEMORIES WERE MADE.

DAY TWENTY-SIX: THANKFULNESS

I once heard a quote that basically said, "It's not happy people who are thankful, it's thankful people who are happy." I couldn't agree more. A thankful heart is exactly what God is looking for and pleased in. When we are thankful it brings Him glory and us joy. In fact, the Bible even says that thankfulness is the will of God (1 Thessalonians 5:18)! A lot of times we think the will of God is this mystical thing like what joy we are to take or what passion we should pursue-when the Bible says just being thankful is His will.

I've seen this to be true in my relationship with Alyssa. I'm serving her the best, loving her the best, and being fulfilled the most in our relationship when I'm thankful...and on the hunt for things to be thankful for.

David Strong shows us how it's done: *"I have tried to be generous in verbalizing my gratitude for all the balls Kristen has juggled and all the hats she had to wear throughout my military career. Every spouse wants his/her contribution to be valued. We can assume our spouse knows how we feel or we can take the time to tell her. She has said how nice it is to hear my gratitude verbally expressed now and then."*

So thankfulness and gratitude are the tasks for today. Specifically list out—and be generous as David said—all the ways you are thankful for your wife or girlfriend. Be sure to include gratitude for her actions, her attitudes, her abilities. Don't skimp. Lavish her with gratitude. Share them with her, for sure, but also keep your list in a place you can see so that you can cultivate an attitude of gratitude for her, which is the will of God!

JOURNAL BELOW:

WRITE WHAT YOU LEARNED TODAY, HOW IT
WENT AND WHAT MEMORIES WERE MADE.

_____

_____

_____

_____

_____

_____

_____

_____

_____

_____

_____

_____

_____

DAY TWENTY-SEVEN: WEEKLY JOURNAL

One of my favorite things Alyssa and I do every week is we get away for about an hour and go through what we call our "marriage journal." Alyssa's parents watch the kiddos and we head off to the beach or somewhere restful and go through the journal. It's a journal we keep that has 5-7 questions we ask ourselves every week and then record the answers in there. It's really enhanced our communication, squashed certain issues before they turn big, and helped us understand more about each other. Also, it's fun to have a written record of our relationship and how we are learning and growing in different seasons.

We got the idea and questions from a friend and have loved doing it ever since. You can use these questions or create your own. The questions we ask are:

1. What brought you joy this week?
2. What's something that was hard this week?
3. What's one specific thing I can do for you this week?
4. How can I pray for you this week?
5. Is there anything that's gone unsaid this week?
6. What's a dream or thought that's been on the forefront of your mind this week?

And then once a month we ask ourselves how our finances and sex life are doing. In all honesty, it's been life changing for us to do this journal. I get to hear how Alyssa's week has been hard when maybe before I wasn't paying attention so well. Also I get to hear how I can serve her in the week ahead.

Army couple, Jacob and Forrest Maechler, offer this encouragement: *"Make conversations—phone calls and video chats—more intentional. Have a list of topics ready to talk about and approach the conversation like you're sitting at dinner together."*

Start keeping a weekly journal—even if it's bullet points—especially if you are away. Your journals can be something you refer to when you do have those rare times to talk or email. It will remind you of funny moments in your week or topics you want to discuss or a future dream you're mulling over. The journals will help you, like they do for Alyssa and me, make conversations more meaningful and intentional.

JOURNAL BELOW:

WRITE WHAT YOU LEARNED TODAY, HOW IT
WENT AND WHAT MEMORIES WERE MADE.

_____

_____

_____

_____

_____

_____

_____

_____

_____

_____

_____

_____

DAY TWENTY-EIGHT: MARK THE MONTHS

Alyssa and I love surprising each other with small (or big) gestures of kindness or gratitude that the other isn't expecting. Sometimes a surprise just says, "Hey I'm thinking about you!" Sometimes we leave little surprises for each other on the bathroom mirror or in each other's car.

When you're separated, you don't always have the luxury of spontaneity, but you can plan surprises ahead of time. For each month you are going to be gone, leave a wrapped surprise with your wife or girlfriend. Tell her she is not allowed to open her surprise until the new month arrives. If you think she'll cheat, leave the surprises with a trusted friend who will deliver them to her one at a time.

In the boxes or bags, leave a handwritten note—it doesn't have to be long. Even just a sticky note (you know how I feel about sticky notes) saying something you love about her. And also leave a gift: a gift card to her favorite ice cream shop, a book by an author she loves, a coffee mug with a funny saying on it, a special candle, movie tickets for her and a friend.

Think of things *she* loves—the more specific the better—as the thought behind the gift, the fact that you really know her, will translate love to her as much as the gift itself. Additionally, this gives her something to look forward to as you mark the months you're apart.

JOURNAL BELOW:

WRITE WHAT YOU LEARNED TODAY, HOW IT
WENT AND WHAT MEMORIES WERE MADE.

DAY TWENTY-NINE: MAKE HOME-COMINGS INTENTIONAL

Homecomings can be, even unknowingly, loaded with huge expectations. One of the best things you can do to avoid miscommunication, disappointment, and frustration, is to talk through your plans well before homecoming happens.

Some of you have girls that like surprises. I know I do! But with everything going on during a homecoming, too many surprises can feel overwhelming. Don't assume anything. Err on the side of talking out expectations, desires, needs, and intentions, even down to small details. For example, do you want other people with you at the initial homecoming? Is there a meal you want or a place you want to go right away?

And don't let the discussion end with the initial reuniting. Keep talking about your expectations for re-entry and the immediate season following your reunion. Talk through resources your branch or command offers to ease the burden of re-entry. Rich and Nicole Schmaeling have learned to take advantage of "POM leave" (pre-deployment and post-deployment leave) and try to get an overnight away without kids.

The Strongs shared a unique experience that helped them: "*David deployed when we were stationed in Hawaii and he had to in-process on a different island from where we lived, which he had to do it before getting home. A friend graciously volunteered to keep our 3 young kids so I could hop islands and meet him. That was unusual, I think, to be able to meet him alone first. Maybe even a luxury. But it is something meaningful that stands out to him.*"

There is no right or wrong way to enjoy homecoming and re-entry. It doesn't matter how anyone else is doing it; choose the right way for you and your marriage and family. You never need to apologize for prioritizing your relationship, especially during intense times of transition. Take note of what works well and what doesn't! And above all, even if things go completely sideways, remember Day 22—GRACE WINS!

JOURNAL BELOW:

WRITE WHAT YOU LEARNED TODAY, HOW IT
WENT AND WHAT MEMORIES WERE MADE.

_____

_____

_____

_____

_____

_____

_____

_____

_____

_____

_____

_____

_____

DAY THIRTY: SCRIP-TURE

Scripture is such a powerful thing. It is active, living, and God's very own word. Scripture can breathe life into a relationship when that relationship comes into contact with it and submits itself to it.

For Alyssa and me, Scripture is everything. Both of us try to read at least a few minutes each day (even though with two young kids that is a tough task). It anchors our relationship and reminds us of what's important and what matters. Ultimately the closer I follow Jesus, the more capacity I have to serve my wife. And the more I drift from Jesus, the more I realize I'm not loving and serving my wife as well.

> *Husbands, go all out in your love for your wives,*
> *exactly as Christ did for the church—*
> *a love marked by giving, not getting.*
> Ephesians 5:25, The Message

A marriage or relationship that prioritizes Scripture as a center point is one that will flourish.

Today find a Scripture passage that you want to dwell on for the next month, something that speaks into your relationship. It can be a verse you want to remind yourself of in order to serve your wife or girlfriend better or it can be one you both agree on as your "relationship verse" for the next month. First Corinthians 13—also known as the "love chapter"— offers a humbling and comprehensive look at what love is and what love does. It's a perfect place to start!

JOURNAL BELOW:

WRITE WHAT YOU LEARNED TODAY, HOW IT
WENT AND WHAT MEMORIES WERE MADE.

DAY THIRTY-ONE: RENEW YOUR MIND

Romans 12:2 says: "Don't copy the behavior and customs of this world, but let God transform you into a new person **by changing the way you think**. Then you will learn to know God's will for you, which is good and pleasing and perfect" (NLT). Other translations say that we must allow God to "renew our mind."

The Message says it this way: "Fix your attention on God. You'll be changed from the inside out."

Our minds are incredibly powerful. It's too easy to think of all the things you'd like to be different right? Unfortunately, this is really easy to do when it comes to your relationship and the unique challenges and stresses of military life. When we allow our minds to roam, undisciplined, we often end up in toxic places. And this kind of thinking has a momentum to it that not only brings us down but it will bring our relationship down too.

Army newlyweds, Caleb and Emily Grow, recently PCS-ed to Germany and they were both struggling with all the changes in their lives. Everything was new. They could have turned away from each other, become negative, but they chose to sit down and pray together—*even when "we didn't feel like it,"* they said.

Forrest and Jacob Maechler recommend writing out a prayer in these times when your mind has gotten away from you. I love this idea! Prayer is an incredible way that we can ask God to renew our minds, changing them from toxic to thankful. Write a prayer today asking God to help you "fix your attention on him" and to "transform the way you think."

We often cannot muster the discipline to turn off all those toxic voices in our heads, wandering thoughts, and unhealthy patterns. We need the power of God in us. Don't be afraid to ask God for his truth, and trust him for a fresh perspective. Your circumstances may not change, but your response to your circumstances can!

JOURNAL BELOW:

WRITE WHAT YOU LEARNED TODAY, HOW IT
WENT AND WHAT MEMORIES WERE MADE.

DAY THIRTY-TWO: YOUR TURN

You didn't think there was going to be a day 32 did ya? We thought we'd add one more day, to turn it over to you. Think of any idea, any gesture, or any kind thing you can do for your significant other today. Be creative. Be loving. And most of all show them how much you care. Also, we'd love to hear what you picked for day 32! We might even end up including it in future versions or volumes of this book. You can upload your idea at *31creativeways.com/upload.* We can't wait to hear how creative you guys are and what y'all came up with!

JOURNAL BELOW:

WRITE WHAT YOU LEARNED TODAY, HOW IT WENT AND WHAT MEMORIES WERE MADE.

_____

_____

_____

_____

_____

_____

_____

A NOTE FROM US AFTER FINISHING THIS BOOK.

First off, you all rock! For reals. Complete rockstars. Why? Because you care about your relationship. You're investing in it. You believe in it. It matters to you.

We believe that a relationship is like a garden. For it to flourish it needs proper nourishment, constant care, pruning, and an awareness of the things trying to invade it. Not to mention gardens, like relationships, can sometimes be a little messy! We hope you'll see this book as just the beginning of a consistent effort to tend to your relationship in nourishing and creative ways.

So thank you for taking this journey with us. Thank you for reading this book. And thank you for just being you. We'd love to hear from you and how the daily challenges went by sharing something online with the hashtag #31creativeways. Be sure and let us know you're a military couple and how you've incorporated any or all of the ideas from this edition. We are constantly on that hashtag to see all the awesome stuff you guys are doing, ways you've tweaked one of our challenges to make it better, and—of course—to get a front row seat to all the fun you're having!

LEARN MORE
ABOUT OUR
AMAZING
MILITARY
CONTRIBUTORS:

LEEANA TANKERSLEY

This project would not have happened without Leeana. We reached out to Leeana early on with an idea for this project after receiving so many messages from couples who were serving in the military. Leeana was the one who made all these wonderful connections for us. Leeana holds English degrees from Liberty University and West Virginia University and is the author of four books, including *Begin Again*. She is married to Steve Tankersley, who is active duty Navy, and they are currently stationed in San Diego, California, with their three kids Luke, Lane, and Elle. Learn more about Leeana at **www.leeanatankersley.com**

MATTHEW & KRISTA COLTER

Matthew and Krista met in June 2014, a little over a year after Matthew joined the Navy. He was stationed in Groton, CT at the Groton Sub base going to school. Krista, born and raised in CT, had just returned home from her freshman year at Cedarville University in Ohio. They were introduced by mutual friends and hit it off immediately.

Three weeks after they met, Matthew was scheduled to be sent to San Diego as his first official duty station. Krista and Matthew were young, he was 23 and she was 19, but they quickly decided their relationship was worth pursuing and decided they would try long distance. During that following year, Matthew went from San Diego to Guam to Hawaii. Krista flew out to Hawaii after the school year ended to visit him. Matthew asked her to marry him during that visit and they eloped that summer.

For the last 2 ½ years, Matthew's current boat has been undergoing repairs and updates, so he has not had the demanding schedule of an operational submarine, which is generally out to sea about 9 months out of the year. They have had one 6-month deployment so far.

In a couple of weeks, the Colter's will learn where the Navy is sending them next. They are so excited to see where their next "home" will be and trust that the Lord will use them wherever the Navy sends them.

CALEB & EMILY GROW

Caleb and Emily have been married since November 23rd, 2016. They met in college at Liberty University in Virginia and were good friends for a while.

They were stationed at Fort Benning in Georgia for about 10 months while Caleb was in IBOLC (Infantry Basic Officer Leadership Course). He is an Infantry Officer in the Army. They moved to Germany recently and will be there for 3 years. Although it's been a big adjustment, they are so excited to travel Europe together.

DAVID & BECKY HAMMOND

As high school sweethearts turned college couple, David and Becky Hammond vowed to clip coupons and live in a shoebox so they could begin their journey of growing up together. After 18 years, Becky has learned to listen instead of take notes as David dreams, while David has become adept at clearing the kitchen to access the most tender parts of Becky's heart.

They have chased adventure and chosen the unconventional together through David's role in the Navy JAG Corps and Becky's pursuit of fueling life-change through people's brilliant Strengths. They are currently in the trenches of life with Littles and are often caught off guard by both the depravity and levity their kids inject into their world. They have four kids— three of whom were born into David's arms and one he welcomed with tears over video from the Middle East.

RICO & HEATHER MADAFFARI

Rico and Heather have been married a little over ten years. They have been blessed with three beautiful children, ages 8, 4, and 2. Throughout their marriage, they have lived in San Diego as well as four of those 10 years in Virginia. They have gone through 7 deployments together and are currently working on their 8th! Although deployments and the military life in general bring challenges, Heather and Rico both say it has also brought them closer and created an even deeper love. They continue to grow and thrive through God's grace.

JACOB & FORREST MAECHLER

Jacob and Forrest Maechler have been a part of the military for almost three years. Jacob is a 1st Lieutenant Chemical officer in the United States Army, and Forrest is currently in nursing school. They are currently serving in Alaska at the Joint Base Elmendorf-Richardson for the next three years and were at Ft. Leonard Wood before that. They have an 8-month old named Jonah, who is all kinds of wonderful!

DAVID & KRISTEN STRONG

Kristen and her United States Air Force veteran husband, David, have 3 children: twin sons (age 18) and a not-a-twin daughter (age 14). Together this former military family zigzagged across the country (and one ocean) several times. Today Kristen and her family enjoy their home under the blue skies of Colorado.

MELISSA REYES & BOYFRIEND, CORY*

Melissa and Cory are from opposite ends of California. They met in Tacoma, Washington through the Army. Cory is on active duty, and Melissa is now in the reserves. They've been in a relationship for 3 years, 2 ½ of it being long distance. Their military relationship is teaching them that relationships aren't cookie cutter perfect, but they are "your own kind of perfect." It's about finding new ways to communicate, trust, respect and love one another, and above all have fun. No day is promised and every day is a blessing.

For security purposes, Cory has chosen to only use his first name.

RICH & NICOLE SCHMAELING

Three states, two countries, 6 moves, 3 kids, 5 deployments, and lots of learning...the life of a military family. Making new friends, grieving the good-byes, and choosing to start again. Nicole says she's thankful for Rich, whom she married 13 years ago. It's amazing for them to see, through the ups and downs, how they continue to be drawn together, challenged, and reminded of God's faithfulness.

Navy life began in San Diego and has brought them coast-to-coast, currently landing them in Italy. Nicole and Rich are grateful for the loving community and friends they've developed along the way, truly the sustenance throughout the long seasons of separation. Choosing outside support when needed, they are stronger for the challenging seasons brought on by life in the military, holding fast to God's promises, He will never leave us nor forsake us. They write, "We give him our mustard seeds of faith, He gives us the feast of His bounty, multiplying the loaves and fishes."

BRIAN & MEGHAN WITTHOEFT

Brian and Meghan have been married over 14 years. They have 5 kids, ages 2-10, and are currently stationed in Naples, Italy. Brian is a Major in the Air Force currently working in the Staff Advisory Group as a Staff Officer at Allied Joint Force Command Naples. Meghan homeschools their children and attempts to manage their busy lives.

After high school Brian enlisted in the Air Force and after training was stationed in Misawa, Japan. It was there he had a supervisor encourage him to apply for a scholarship and the Reserve Officer Training Corps program.

Brian and Meghan met at Iowa State University during their freshman year. They were married in 2003, just a week after finishing their junior year. Since then, the Witthoefts have been in Ohio, graduate school, Florida, back to Iowa, California, Montana, and now in Italy. They have also survived a 4-days-notice deployment to Afghanistan!

For those who maybe are getting this as a gift or don't know much about us, below are just a few other things we have created and done over the past few years. **We hope they encourage you!**

WHERE TO FIND US ONLINE.

We love when folks give us a shout on social media, so feel free to stop by and say hey! Would love to e-meet you.

INSTAGRAM

@jeffersonbethke
@alyssajoybethke

TWITTER

@jeffersonbethke
@alyssajoybethke

FACEBOOK

fb.com/jeffersonbethkepage
fb.com/alyssajoybethke

SNAPCHAT
Username: jeffersonbethke

WEBSITES

jeffandalyssa.com
lovethatlasts.co
31creativeways.com

STORE

Shop.jeffandalyssa.com

We are always looking for great things to help marriages and relationships. We've found a few we absolutely love and hope you guys will too!

DATEBOX:

We LOVE this. It's a subscription service that sends you a fully curated Datebox every month to your doorstep. For example, during the Christmas season in December we got a box that included a gingerbread making kit, two custom mugs, hot cocoa mix, a Christmas playlist and bunch more goodies. We have a blast every time one shows up on our door. We wanted to hook you guys up to check it out. If you use code 'bethke' at checkout at **http://www.getdatebox.com**, you get your first month 50% off. Definitely a steal of a deal and something we love!

Strongermarriages.com: This is a phenomenal website that has crazy amounts of content to help and build any marriage out there! They have courses, blogs, books and more. It's a site that isn't afraid to talk about real life either, which is so important to us.